Our Mother Earth

POPE FRANCIS

Our Mother Earth

A Christian Reading of the Challenge of the Environment

WITH A PREFACE BY
ECUMENICAL PATRIARCH BARTHOLOMEW

Our Sunday Visitor
Huntington, Indiana

Published in English by Our Sunday Visitor Publishing Division, Our Sunday Visitor, Inc., 200 Noll Plaza, Huntington, IN 46750; 1-800-348-2440; www.osv.com.

ISBN: 978-1-68192-669-8 (Inventory No. T2536)

1. RELIGION—Christianity —Catholic.

2. RELIGION—Christian Living—Prayer.

3. RELIGION—Christian Living—Inspirational.

eISBN: 978-1-68192-670-4

LCCN: 2020939794

Cover design: Amanda Falk

Cover art: Adobe Stock

Interior design: Amanda Falk

PRINTED IN THE UNITED STATES OF AMERICA

CONTENTS

PREFACE

+ *Bartholomew*
Archbishop of Constantinople — New
Rome and Ecumenical Patriarch

When, in a gesture of spontaneous ecumenical solidarity, we decided to attend the inauguration Mass of Pope Francis in March 2013, we could not have imagined the infinite dimensions of faithful ministry to the principles and precepts of the Gospel that would emerge as the result of our fraternity and friendship.

Of course, we were deeply convinced of the significance and sacredness of our efforts at dialogue in love and truth in order to restore our unity and communion as disciples of the Lord, who prayed that we might be one (cf. Jn 17:21), and we were passionately engaged in it. Yet we could not have imagined the global repercussions of an authentic service on behalf of human rights and social justice that would arise from our love and concern for God's creation.

Just one year later, in May 2014, we began a joint pilgrimage to Jerusalem with Pope Francis in order to commemorate and celebrate the fifty years since our venerable predecessors, Ecumenical Patriarch Athenagoras and Pope Paul VI, met there in 1964. While the context of the event was ecumenical, the focus was on religious persecution and suffering in the Middle East. Meetings of prayer and peace in the same spirit followed in Vatican City (2014), Istanbul (2014), Assisi (2016), Cairo (2017), and Bari (2018). In the Holy Land we also jointly declared the following:

> Yet even as we make this journey toward full communion we already have the duty to offer common witness to the love of God for all people by working together in the service of humanity ... in promoting peace and the common good, and in responding to the suffering that continues to afflict our world. ... It is our profound conviction that the future of the human family depends also on how we safeguard — both prudently and compassionately, with justice and fairness — the gift of creation that our Creator has entrusted to us. ... We express our shared profound concern for the situation of Christians in the Middle East and for their right to remain full citizens of their homelands. ... We are persuaded that it is not

arms, but dialogue, pardon and reconciliation that are the only possible means to achieve peace.[1]

In April 2016 we met Pope Francis and Archbishop Ierony-mos of Athens on the Greek island of Lesbos, near the Turk-ish coast, to personally meet the refugees who risked their lives by crossing the Aegean Sea to escape persecution and poverty and reach Europe. Many lost their lives and their families during the journey. We have expressed our solidar-ity and support for their protection and safety and for their rights. We also issued a Joint Declaration on the moral obli-gation to receive these refugees, in which we stated:

> World opinion cannot ignore the colossal humanitarian crisis created by the spread of violence and armed con-flict, the persecution and displacement of religious and ethnic minorities, and the uprooting of families from their homes, in violation of their human dignity and their fundamental human rights and freedoms.
>
> The tragedy of forced migration and displacement affects millions, and is fundamentally a crisis of hu-manity, calling for a response of solidarity, compassion, generosity and an immediate practical commitment of resources. … We appeal to the international community to respond with courage in facing this massive human-itarian crisis and its underlying causes, through diplo-matic, political and charitable initiatives, and through cooperative efforts, both in the Middle East and in Eu-rope.[2]

In September 2017, on the World Day of Prayer for the Care of Creation, celebrated by the Ecumenical Patriarchate since 1989, Pope Francis and Our Humble Person drew up a historic Joint Declaration on the sacredness of God's creation and the importance of its protection by us human beings. Two years after the publication of Pope Francis' *Laudato Si'*, we solemnly declared to the Christian faithful as well as to political leaders:

> The impact of climate change affects, first and foremost, those who live in poverty in every corner of the globe. Our obligation to use the earth's goods responsibly implies the recognition of and respect for all people and all living creatures. The urgent call and challenge to care for creation are an invitation for all of humanity to work toward sustainable and integral development. ... We are convinced that there can be no sincere and enduring resolution to the challenge of the ecological crisis and climate change unless the response is concerted and collective, unless the responsibility is shared and accountable, unless we give priority to solidarity and service.[3]

In recent years much has happened within our churches as well as bilaterally between the Orthodox Church and the Roman Catholic Church. Thus we have learned that there is a close link between ecumenical dialogue and care for the environment. We have come to realize that, alongside the ecumenism of dialogue between the various Christian denominations and the ecumenism of martyrdom shared by the victims of religious discrimination and violence, there is also an ecumenism of the environment in the face of global climate change that brings with it far-reaching implications and consequences for our entire planet and its inhabitants.

This means that we can never reduce Christian life and Christian service to our small interests or spiritual concerns. We cannot neglect our task and responsibility to transform creation through the questioning and transforming of our selfish lifestyles and our greedy consumption of the world's resources. The way we relate to material things directly reflects the way we relate to God. And the attention with which we treat things on earth clearly shows the sacredness we ascribe to heavenly realities. This is not only a matter for us as individuals, but also as a community and society as a whole.

The truth is that we must treat nature with the same deference and admiration we show for human beings. To remedy this situation, we are called to return to an ascetic and Eucharistic lifestyle — that is, to be thankful by offering glory to God for the gift of creation and at the same time respectful in the exercise of our personal responsibility within and for the web of relationships of creation. We are called to constantly remind ourselves that our world economy is simply becoming too large for our planet's capacity to maintain and sustain it.

Moreover, our attitudes and behavior toward creation directly affect and are reflected in our attitudes and behavior toward other people. Indeed, our work in the field of ecology is ultimately measured by its effect on people, especially the poor. And a Church that forgets to pray for the natural environment is a Church that refuses to offer food and drink to suffering humanity. At the same time, a society that ignores the mandate to care for all people is a society that mistreats God's authentic creation, of which nature is part. After all, concern for the environment also implies concern for the human problems of poverty, hunger, and thirst. This bond is strongly emphasized in the parable of the Last Judgment, when the Lord says, "I was hungry and you gave me food, I was thirsty and you gave me something to drink" (Mt 25:35).

The source of our optimism, however, lies in the fact that we are not alone in our response and responsibility for the protection of human dignity and the protection of God's creation. Not only is there the certainty of the Lord's grace, but we also have the solidarity of our brothers and sisters. This is what we have learned from our relationship with our beloved Pope Francis, with whom we share a commitment to the hope of all peoples and a joy for the healing of our planet.

As servants of the God of love, we consider that one of our fundamental obligations and moral duties is to respond to global suffering and bequeath to future generations a sustainable world, as created and willed by our loving Creator.

An Integral Vision

A GLOBAL COLLABORATION

The[1] urgent challenge to protect our common home includes a concern to bring the whole human family together to seek a sustainable and integral development, for we know that things can change. The Creator does not abandon us; he never forsakes his loving plan or repents of having created us. Humanity still has the ability to work together in building our common home. Here I want to recognize, encourage, and thank all those striving in countless ways to guarantee the protection of the home which we share. Particular appreciation is owed to those who tirelessly seek to resolve the tragic effects of environmental degradation on the lives of the world's poorest. Young people demand change. They wonder how anyone can claim to be building a better future without thinking of the environmental crisis and the sufferings of the excluded.

THE VALUE OF LABOR

Any[2] approach to an integral ecology, which by definition does not exclude human beings, needs to take account of the value of labor, as Saint John Paul II wisely noted in his encyclical *Laborem Exercens*. According to the biblical account of creation, God placed man and woman in the garden he had created (cf. Gn 2:15) not only to preserve it ("keep") but also to make it fruitful ("till"). Laborers and craftsmen thus "maintain the fabric of the world" (Sir 38:34). Developing the created world in a prudent way is the best way of caring for it, as this means that we ourselves become the instrument used by God to bring out the potential which he himself inscribed in things: "The Lord created medicines out of the earth, and a sensible man will not despise them" (Sir 38:4).

SAFEGUARDING WHAT OUR CHILDREN HAVE LOANED TO US

The[3] earth was entrusted to us in order that it be mother for us, capable of giving to each one what is necessary to live. I once heard something beautiful: the earth is not an inheritance that we receive from our parents, but a loan that our children give to us, in order that we safeguard it, and make it flourish, and return it to them. The earth is generous and holds back nothing from those who safeguard it. The earth, which is mother of all, asks for respect, not violence or, worse yet, arrogance from masters. We must return it to our children improved, safeguarded, for they have loaned it to us. The attitude of safeguarding is not the exclusive duty of Christians, it is everyone's.

From Momentous Challenge to Global Opportunity

POLLUTION AND CLIMATE CHANGE

The[1] climate is a common good, belonging to all and meant for all. At the global level, it is a complex system linked to many of the essential conditions for human life. A very solid scientific consensus indicates that we are presently witnessing a disturbing warming of the climatic system. In recent decades this warming has been accompanied by a constant rise in the sea level and, it would appear, by an increase of extreme weather events, even if a scientifically determinable cause cannot be assigned to each particular phenomenon. Humanity is called to recognize the need for changes of lifestyle, production, and consumption, in order to combat this warming or at least the human causes which produce or aggravate it. It is true that there are other factors (such as volcanic activity, variations in the earth's orbit and axis, the solar cycle), yet a number of scientific studies indicate that most global warming in recent decades is due to the great concentration of greenhouse gases (carbon dioxide, methane, nitrogen oxides, and others) released mainly as a result of human activity. As these gases build up in the atmosphere, they hamper the escape of heat produced by sunlight at the earth's surface. The problem is aggravated by a model of development based on the intensive use of fossil fuels, which is at the heart of the worldwide energy system. Another determining factor has been an increase in changed uses of the soil, principally deforestation for agricultural purposes.

Warming has effects on the carbon cycle. It creates a vicious circle which aggravates the situation even more, affecting the availability of essential resources like drinking water, energy, and agricultural production in warmer regions, and leading to the extinction of part of the planet's biodiversity. The melting in the polar ice caps and in high altitude plains can lead to the dangerous release of methane gas, while the decomposition of frozen organic material can further increase the emission of carbon dioxide. Things are made worse by the loss of tropical forests which would otherwise help to mitigate climate change. Carbon dioxide pollution increases the acidification of the oceans and compromises the marine food chain. If present trends continue, this century may well witness extraordinary climate change and an unprecedented destruction of ecosystems, with serious consequences for all of us. A rise in the sea level, for example, can create extremely serious situations, if we consider that a quarter of the world's population lives on the coast or nearby, and that the majority of our megacities are situated in coastal areas.

Climate change is a global problem with grave implications: environmental, social, economic, political, and for the distribution of goods. It represents one of the principal challenges facing humanity in our day. Its worst impact will probably be felt by developing countries in coming decades. Many of the poor live in areas particularly affected by phenomena related to warming, and their means of subsistence are largely dependent on natural reserves and ecosystemic services such as agriculture, fishing, and forestry. They have no other financial activities or resources which can enable them to adapt to climate change or to face natural disasters, and their access to social services and protection is very limited. For example, changes in climate, to which animals and plants cannot adapt, lead them to migrate; this in turn affects the livelihood of the poor, who are then forced to leave their homes, with great uncertainty for their future and that of their children. There has been a tragic rise in the number of migrants seeking to flee from the growing poverty caused by environmental degradation. They are not recognized by international conventions as refugees; they bear the loss of the lives they have left behind, without enjoying any legal protection whatsoever. Sadly, there is widespread indifference to such suffering, which is even now taking place throughout our world. Our lack of response to these tragedies involving our brothers and sisters points to the loss of that sense of responsibility for our fellow men and women upon which all civil society is founded.

Many of those who possess more resources and economic or political power seem mostly to be concerned with masking the problems or concealing their symptoms, simply making efforts to reduce some of the negative impacts of climate change. However, many of these symptoms indicate that such effects will continue to worsen if we continue with current models of production and consumption. There is an urgent need to develop policies so that, in the next few years, the emission of carbon dioxide and other highly polluting gases can be drastically reduced — for example, substituting for fossil fuels and developing sources of renewable energy. Worldwide there is minimal access to clean and renewable energy. There is still a need to develop adequate storage technologies. Some countries have made considerable progress, although it is far from constituting a significant proportion. Investments have also been made in means of production and transportation which consume less energy and require fewer raw materials, as well as in methods of construction and renovating buildings which improve their energy efficiency. But these good practices are still far from widespread.

LOSS OF BIODIVERSITY

The[2] earth's resources are also being plundered because of shortsighted approaches to the economy, commerce, and production. The loss of forests and woodlands entails the loss of species which may constitute extremely important resources in the future, not only for food but also for curing disease and other uses. Different species contain genes which could be key resources in years ahead for meeting human needs and regulating environmental problems.

It is not enough, however, to think of different species merely as potential "resources" to be exploited, while overlooking the fact that they have value in themselves. Each year sees the disappearance of thousands of plant and animal species which we will never know, which our children will never see, because they have been lost forever. The great majority become extinct for reasons related to human activity. Because of us, thousands of species will no longer give glory to God by their very existence, nor convey their message to us. We have no such right.

It may well disturb us to learn of the extinction of mammals or birds, since they are more visible. But the good functioning of ecosystems also requires fungi, algae, worms, insects, reptiles, and an innumerable variety of microorganisms. Some less numerous species, although generally unseen, nonetheless play a critical role in maintaining the equilibrium of a particular place. Human beings must intervene when a geosystem reaches a critical state. But nowadays, such intervention in nature has become more and more frequent. As a consequence, serious problems arise, leading to further interventions; human activity becomes ubiquitous, with all the risks which this entails. Often a vicious circle results, as human intervention to resolve a problem further aggravates the situation. For example, many birds and insects which disappear due to synthetic agrotoxins are helpful for agriculture: their disappearance will have to be compensated for by yet other techniques which may well prove harmful. We must be grateful for the praiseworthy efforts being made by scientists and engineers dedicated to finding solutions to man-made problems. But a sober look at our world shows that the degree of human intervention, often in the service of business interests and consumerism, is actually making our earth less rich and beautiful, ever more limited and gray, even as technological advances and consumer goods continue to abound limitlessly. We seem to think that we can substitute an irreplaceable and irretrievable beauty with something which we have created ourselves.

In assessing the environmental impact of any project, concern is usually shown for its effects on soil, water, and air, yet few careful studies are made of its impact on biodiversity, as if the loss of species or animals and plant groups were of little importance. Highways, new plantations, the fencing-off of certain areas, the damming of water sources, and similar developments crowd out natural habitats and, at times, break them up in such a way that animal populations can no longer migrate or roam freely. As a result, some species face extinction. Alternatives exist which at least lessen the impact of these projects, like the creation of biological corridors, but few countries demonstrate such concern and foresight. Frequently, when certain species are exploited commercially, little attention is paid to studying their reproductive patterns in order to prevent their depletion and the consequent imbalance of the ecosystem.

Caring for ecosystems demands farsightedness, since no one looking for quick and easy profit is truly interested in their preservation. But the cost of the damage caused by such selfish lack of concern is much greater than the economic benefits to be obtained. Where certain species are destroyed or seriously harmed, the values involved are incalculable. We can be silent witnesses to terrible injustices if we think that we can obtain significant benefits by making the rest of humanity, present and future, pay the extremely high costs of environmental deterioration.

Some countries have made significant progress in establishing sanctuaries on land and in the oceans where any human intervention is prohibited which might modify their features or alter their original structures. In the protection of biodiversity, specialists insist on the need for particular attention to be shown to areas richer both in the number of species and in endemic, rare, or less protected species. Certain places need greater protection because of their immense importance for the global ecosystem, or because they represent important water reserves and thus safeguard other forms of life.

Let us mention, for example, those richly biodiverse lungs of our planet which are the Amazon and the Congo basins, or the great aquifers and glaciers. We know how important these are for the entire earth and for the future of humanity. The ecosystems of tropical forests possess an enormously complex biodiversity which is almost impossible to appreciate fully, yet when these forests are burned down or leveled for purposes of cultivation, within the space of a few years countless species are lost and the areas frequently become arid wastelands. A delicate balance has to be maintained when speaking about these places, for we cannot overlook the huge global economic interests which, under the guise of protecting them, can undermine the sovereignty of individual nations. In fact, there are "proposals to internationalize the Amazon, which only serve the economic interests of transnational corporations."[3] We cannot fail to praise the commitment of international agencies and civil society organizations which draw public attention to these issues and offer critical cooperation, employing legitimate means of pressure, to ensure that each government carries out its proper and inalienable responsibility to preserve its country's environment and natural resources, without capitulating to spurious local or international interests.

The replacement of virgin forest with plantations of trees, usually monocultures, is rarely adequately analyzed. Yet this can seriously compromise a biodiversity which the new species being introduced does not accommodate. Similarly, wetlands converted into cultivated land lose the enormous biodiversity which they formerly hosted. In some coastal areas the disappearance of ecosystems sustained by mangrove swamps is a source of serious concern.

Oceans not only contain the bulk of our planet's water supply, but also most of the immense variety of living creatures, many of them still unknown to us and threatened for various reasons. What is more, marine life in rivers, lakes, seas, and oceans, which feeds a great part of the world's population, is affected by uncontrolled fishing, leading to a drastic depletion of certain species. Selective forms of fishing which discard much of what they collect continue unabated. Particularly threatened are marine organisms which we tend to overlook, like some forms of plankton; they represent a significant element in the ocean food chain, and species used for our food ultimately depend on them.

In tropical and subtropical seas, we find coral reefs comparable to the great forests on dry land, for they shelter approximately a million species, including fish, crabs, molluscs, sponges, and algae. Many of the world's coral reefs are already barren or in a state of constant decline. "Who turned the wonderworld of the seas into underwater cemeteries bereft of color and life?"[4] This phenomenon is due largely to pollution which reaches the sea as the result of deforestation, agricultural monocultures, industrial waste, and destructive fishing methods, especially those using cyanide and dynamite. It is aggravated by the rise in temperature of the oceans. All of this helps us to see that every intervention in nature can have consequences which are not immediately evident, and that certain ways of exploiting resources prove costly in terms of degradation which ultimately reaches the ocean bed itself.

Greater investment needs to be made in research aimed at understanding more fully the functioning of ecosystems and adequately analyzing the different variables associated with any significant modification of the environment. Because all creatures are connected, each must be cherished with love and respect, for all of us as living creatures are dependent on one another. Each area is responsible for the care of this family. This will require undertaking a careful inventory of the species which it hosts, with a view to developing programs and strategies of protection with particular care for safeguarding species heading toward extinction.

EDUCATION TOWARD AN ALLIANCE BETWEEN HUMANITY AND THE ENVIRONMENT

An[5] awareness of the gravity of today's cultural and ecological crisis must be translated into new habits. Many people know that our current progress and the mere amassing of things and pleasures are not enough to give meaning and joy to the human heart, yet they feel unable to give up what the market sets before them. In those countries which should be making the greatest changes in consumer habits, young people have a new ecological sensitivity and a generous spirit, and some of them are making admirable efforts to protect the environment. At the same time, they have grown up in a milieu of extreme consumerism and affluence which makes it difficult to develop other habits. We are faced with an educational challenge.

Environmental education has broadened its goals. Whereas in the beginning it was mainly centered on scientific information, consciousness-raising, and the prevention of environmental risks, it tends now to include a critique of the "myths" of a modernity grounded in a utilitarian mindset (individualism, unlimited progress, competition, consumerism, the unregulated market). It seeks also to restore the various levels of ecological equilibrium, establishing harmony within ourselves, with others, with nature, and other living creatures, and with God. Environmental education should facilitate making the leap toward the transcendent which gives ecological ethics its deepest meaning. It needs educators capable of developing an ethics of ecology and helping people, through effective pedagogy, to grow in solidarity, responsibility, and compassionate care.

Yet this education, aimed at creating an "ecological citizenship," is at times limited to providing information, and fails to instill good habits. The existence of laws and regulations is insufficient in the long run to curb bad conduct, even when effective means of enforcement are present. If the laws are to bring about significant, long-lasting effects, the majority of the members of society must be adequately motivated to accept them, and personally transformed to respond. Only by cultivating sound virtues will people be able to make a selfless ecological commitment. A person who could afford to spend and consume more but regularly uses less heating and wears warmer clothes shows the kind of convictions and attitudes which help to protect the environment. There is a nobility in the duty to care for creation through little daily actions, and it is wonderful how education can bring about real changes in lifestyle. Education in environmental responsibility can encourage ways of acting which directly and significantly affect the world around us, such as "avoiding the use of plastic and paper, reducing water consumption, separating refuse, cooking only what can reasonably be consumed, showing care for other living beings, using public transport or car-pooling, planting trees, turning off unnecessary lights, or any number of other practices" (Laudato Si', 211). All of these reflect a generous and worthy creativity which brings out the best in human beings. Reusing something instead of immediately discarding it, when done for the right reasons, can be an act of love which expresses our own dignity.

We must not think that these efforts are not going to change the world. They benefit society, often unbeknown to us, for they call forth a goodness which, albeit unseen, inevitably tends to spread. Furthermore, such actions can restore our sense of self-esteem; they can enable us to live more fully and to feel that life on earth is worthwhile.

Ecological education can take place in a variety of settings: at school, in families, in the media, in catechesis, and elsewhere. Good education plants seeds when we are young, and these continue to bear fruit throughout life. Here, though, I would stress the great importance of the family, which is

> the place in which life — the gift of God — can be properly welcomed and protected against the many attacks to which it is exposed, and can develop in accordance with what constitutes authentic human growth. In the face of the so-called culture of death, the family is the heart of the culture of life.[6]

In the family we first learn how to show love and respect for life; we are taught the proper use of things, order and cleanliness, respect for the local ecosystem, and care for all creatures. In the family we receive an integral education, which enables us to grow harmoniously in personal maturity. In the family we learn to ask without demanding, to say "thank you" as an expression of genuine gratitude for what we have been given, to control our aggressivity and greed, and to ask forgiveness when we have caused harm. These simple gestures of heartfelt courtesy help to create a culture of shared life and respect for our surroundings.

Political institutions and various other social groups are also entrusted with helping to raise people's awareness. So, too, is the Church. All Christian communities have an important role to play in ecological education. It is my hope that our seminaries and houses of formation will provide an education in responsible simplicity of life, in grateful contemplation of God's world, and in concern for the needs of the poor and the protection of the environment. Because the stakes are so high, we need institutions empowered to impose penalties for damage inflicted on the environment. But we also need the personal qualities of self-control and willingness to learn from one another.

In this regard, "the relationship between a good aesthetic education and the maintenance of a healthy environment cannot be overlooked."[7] By learning to see and appreciate beauty, we learn to reject self-interested pragmatism. If someone has not learned to stop and admire something beautiful, we should not be surprised if he or she treats everything as an object to be used and abused without scruple. If we want to bring about deep change, we need to realize that certain mindsets really do influence our behavior. Our efforts at education will be inadequate and ineffectual unless we strive to promote a new way of thinking about human beings, life, society, and our relationship with nature. Otherwise, the paradigm of consumerism will continue to advance, with the help of the media and the highly effective workings of the market.

Speeches, Audiences, and Homilies

LET US PROTECT CHRIST IN OUR LIVES

Let us protect[1] Christ in our lives, to protect others, to protect creation!

The vocation of being a "protector," however, is not just something involving us Christians alone; it also has a prior dimension which is simply human, involving everyone. It means protecting all creation, the beauty of the created world, as the Book of Genesis tells us and as Saint Francis of Assisi showed us. It means respecting each of God's creatures and respecting the environment in which we live. It means protecting people, showing loving concern for each and every person, especially children, the elderly, those in need, who are often the last we think about. It means caring for one another in our families: husbands and wives first protect one another, and then, as parents, they care for their children, and children themselves, in time, protect their parents. It means building sincere friendships in which we protect one another in trust, respect, and goodness. In the end, everything has been entrusted to our protection, and all of us are responsible for it. Be protectors of God's gifts!

Whenever human beings fail to live up to this responsibility, whenever we fail to care for creation and for our brothers and sisters, the way is opened to destruction and hearts are hardened. Tragically, in every period of history there are "Herods" who plot death, wreak havoc, and mar the countenance of men and women.

Please, I would like to ask all those who have positions of responsibility in economic, political, and social life, and all men and women of goodwill: Let us be "protectors" of creation, protectors of God's plan inscribed in nature, protectors of one another and of the environment. Let us not allow omens of destruction and death to accompany the advance of this world! But to be "protectors," we also have to keep watch over ourselves! Let us not forget that hatred, envy, and pride defile our lives! Being protectors, then, also means keeping watch over our emotions, over our hearts, because they are the seat of good and evil intentions: intentions that build up and tear down! We must not be afraid of goodness or even tenderness!

Here I would add one more thing: caring, protecting, demands goodness, it calls for a certain tenderness. In the Gospels, Saint Joseph appears as a strong and courageous man, a working man, yet in his heart we see great tenderness, which is not the virtue of the weak but rather a sign of strength of spirit and a capacity for concern, for compassion, for genuine openness to others, for love. We must not be afraid of goodness, of tenderness!

Today, together with the feast of Saint Joseph, we are celebrating the beginning of the ministry of the new Bishop of Rome, the Successor of Peter, which also involves a certain power. Certainly, Jesus Christ conferred power upon Peter, but what sort of power was it? Jesus' three questions to Peter about love are followed by three commands: feed my lambs, feed my sheep. Let us never forget that authentic power is service, and that the pope, too, when exercising power, must enter ever more fully into that service which has its radiant culmination on the cross. He must be inspired by the lowly, concrete, and faithful service which marked Saint Joseph, and, like him, he must open his arms to protect all of God's people and embrace with tender affection the whole of humanity, especially the poorest, the weakest, the least important, those whom Matthew lists in the final judgment on love: the hungry, the thirsty, the stranger, the naked, the sick, and those in prison (cf. Mt 25:31–46). Only those who serve with love are able to protect!

In the second reading, Saint Paul speaks of Abraham, who, "hoping against hope, believed" (Rom 4:18). Hoping against hope! Today, too, amid so much darkness, we need to see the light of hope and to be men and women who bring hope to others. To protect creation, to protect every man and every woman, to look upon them with tenderness and love, is to open up a horizon of hope; it is to let a shaft of light break through the heavy clouds; it is to bring the warmth of hope! For believers, for us Christians, like Abraham, like Saint Joseph, the hope that we bring is set against the horizon of God, which has opened up before us in Christ. It is a hope built on the rock which is God.

To protect Jesus with Mary, to protect the whole of creation, to protect each person, especially the poorest, to protect ourselves: this is a service that the Bishop of Rome is called to carry out, yet one to which all of us are called, so that the star of hope will shine brightly. Let us protect with love all that God has given us!

CREATION IS GOD'S MOST BEAUTIFUL GIFT

In[2] the first chapter of Genesis, right at the beginning of the Bible, what is emphasized is that God is pleased with his creation, stressing repeatedly the beauty and goodness of every single thing. At the end of each day, it is written: "God saw that it was good" (1:12, 18, 21, 25): if God sees creation as good, as a beautiful thing, then we, too, must take this attitude and see that creation is a good and beautiful thing. Now, this is the gift of knowledge that allows us to see this beauty, therefore we praise God, giving thanks to him for having granted us so much beauty. And when God finished creating man, he didn't say "he saw that this was good," but said that this was "very good" (v. 31). In the eyes of God we are the most beautiful thing, the greatest, the best of creation: even the angels are beneath us, we are more than the angels, as we heard in the Book of Psalms. The Lord favors us! We must give thanks to him for this. The gift of knowledge sets us in profound *harmony with the Creator* and allows us to participate in the clarity of his vision and his judgment. And it is in this perspective that we manage to accept man and woman as the summit of creation, as the fulfillment of a plan of love that is impressed in each one of us and that allows us to recognize one another as brothers and sisters.

All this is a source of serenity and peace and makes the Christian a joyful witness of God, [following] in the footsteps of Saint Francis of Assisi and so many saints who knew how to praise and laud his love through the contemplation of creation. At the same time, however, the gift of knowledge helps us not to fall into attitudes of excess or error. The first lies in the risk of considering ourselves the masters of creation. Creation is not some possession that we can lord over for our own pleasure; nor, even less, is it the property of only some people, the few: creation is a gift, it is the marvelous gift that God has given us, *so that we will take care of it and harness it for the benefit of all, always with great respect and gratitude.* The second erroneous attitude is represented by the temptation to stop at creatures, as if these could provide the answer to all our expectations. With the gift of knowledge, the Spirit helps us not to fall into this error.

But I would like to return to the first of these incorrect paths: tyranny over, rather than the custody of, creation. We must protect creation for it is a gift which the Lord has given us, it is God's present to us; we are the guardians of creation.

When we exploit creation, we destroy that sign of God's love. To destroy creation is to say to God, "I don't care," And this is not good: this is sin.

Custody of creation is precisely custody of God's gift and it is saying to God, "Thank you, I am the guardian of creation so as to make it progress, never to destroy your gift." This must be our attitude to creation: Guard it, for if we destroy creation, creation will destroy us! Don't forget that. Once I was in the countryside and I heard a saying from a simple person who had a great love for flowers and took care of them. He said to me: "We must take care of the beautiful things that God has given us! Creation is ours so that we can receive good things from it; not exploit it, to protect it. *God forgives always, we men forgive sometimes, but creation never forgives, and if you don't care for it, it will destroy you.*"

This should make us think and should make us ask the Holy Spirit for the gift of knowledge in order to understand better that creation is a most beautiful gift of God. He has done many good things for the thing that is most good: the human person.

CARING FOR HUMAN LIFE, CARING FOR THE PLANET

Mr. President, Ladies and Gentlemen,

I[3] am pleased and honored to speak here today, at this Second International Conference on Nutrition. I wish to thank you, Mr. President, for your warm greeting and words of welcome. I cordially greet the Director General of the FAO, Professor José Graziano da Silva, and the Director General of the World Health Organization (WHO), Dr. Margaret Chan, and I rejoice in their decision to convene to this conference the representatives of states, international institutions, and organizations of civil society, the world of agriculture and the private sector, with the aim of studying together the forms of intervention necessary to assure food security, as well as to insist on the changes that must be made to existing strategies. The concerted unity of purpose and of action, but above all the spirit of brotherhood, can be decisive in finding appropriate solutions. The Church, as you know, always seeks to be attentive and watchful regarding the spiritual and material welfare of people, especially those who are marginalized or excluded, in order to guarantee their safety and dignity.

The future of all nations is interconnected, more than ever before; they are like the members of one family who depend upon each other. However, we live in an era in which relations between nations are all too often damaged by mutual suspicion, which at times turns into forms of military and economic aggression, undermining friendship between brothers and rejecting or emarginating [sic] those who are already excluded. Those who lack their daily bread or decent employment are well aware of this. This is a picture of today's world, in which it is necessary to recognize the limits of approaches based on the sovereignty of each state, understood as absolute, and on national interests, frequently conditioned by small power groups. This is well demonstrated by your working agenda for developing new standards, structures, and greater commitments to feed the world. In this perspective, I hope that, in the formulation of these commitments, states may be inspired by the conviction that the right to nutrition can be guaranteed only if we care about the actual subject, that is, the person who suffers the effects of hunger and malnutrition: the true subject!

Nowadays there is much talk of rights, frequently neglecting duties; perhaps we have paid too little heed to those who are hungry. It is also painful to see that the fight against hunger and malnutrition is hindered by "market priorities," the "primacy of profit," which have reduced foodstuffs to a commodity like any other, subject to speculation, also of a financial nature. And while we speak of new rights, the hungry are waiting, at the street corner, asking for the right to citizenship, asking for due consideration of their status, to receive a healthy, basic diet. They ask for dignity, not for alms.

These criteria cannot remain in the limbo of theory. Individuals and peoples ask that justice be put into practice: not only in the legal sense, but also in terms of contribution and distribution. Therefore, development plans and the work of international organizations must take into consideration the wish, so frequent among ordinary people, for respect for fundamental human rights in all circumstances and, in this case, the rights of the hungry person. When this is achieved, then humanitarian intervention, emergency relief, and development operations — in their truest, fullest sense — will attain greater momentum and yield the desired results.

Interest in the production, availability, and accessibility of foodstuffs in climate change and in agricultural trade should certainly inspire rules and technical measures, but the first concern must be the individual person, who lacks daily nourishment, who has given up thinking about life, family, and social relationships, and instead fights only for survival. At the inauguration of the First Conference on Nutrition in this hall in 1992, Pope Saint John Paul II warned the international community of the risk of the "paradox of abundance," in which there is food for everyone, but not everyone can eat, while waste, excessive consumption, and the use of food for other purposes is visible before our very eyes. This is the paradox! Unfortunately, this "paradox" persists. There are few subjects about which there are as many fallacies as there are about hunger; few topics are as likely to be manipulated by data, statistics, by national security demands, corruption, or by grim references to the economic crisis. This is the first challenge that must be overcome.

The second challenge that must be addressed is the lack of solidarity; subconsciously we suspect that this word should be removed from the dictionary. Our societies are characterized by growing individualism and division: this ends up depriving the weakest of a decent life, and provokes revolts against institutions. When there is a lack of solidarity in a country, the effects are felt by all. Indeed, solidarity is the attitude that enables people to reach out to others and establish mutual relations on this sense of brotherhood that overcomes differences and limits, and inspires us to seek the common good together. Human beings, as they become aware of being partly responsible for the plan of Creation, become capable of mutual respect, instead of fighting among themselves, damaging and impoverishing the planet. States, too, understood as communities of individuals and peoples, are called to act concertedly, to be willing to help each other through the principles and norms offered by international law. An inexhaustible source of inspiration, natural law, is inscribed in the human heart and speaks to everyone in understandable terms: love, justice, peace, elements that are inseparable from each other. Like people, states and international institutions are called to welcome and nurture these values in a spirit of dialogue and mutual listening. In this way, the aim of feeding the human family becomes feasible.

Every woman, man, child, and elderly person everywhere should be able to count on these guarantees. It is the duty of every state that cares for the well-being of its citizens to subscribe to them unreservedly and to take the necessary steps to ensure their implementation. This requires perseverance and support. The Catholic Church also offers her contribution in this field through constant attention to the life of the poor, of the needy in all parts of the world; along the same lines, the Holy See is actively involved in international organizations and through numerous documents and statements. In this way, it contributes to identifying and adopting the criteria to be met in order to develop an equitable international system. These are criteria that, on the ethical plane, are based on the pillars of truth, freedom, justice, and solidarity. At the same time, in the legal field, these same criteria include: the relationship between the right to nutrition and the right to life and to a dignified existence; the right to be protected by law, however, is not always close to the reality of those who suffer from hunger; and the moral obligation to share the world's economic wealth. If we believe in the principle of the unity of the human family, based on the common paternity of God the Creator, and on the fraternity of human beings, no form of political or economic pressure which exploits the availability of foodstuffs can be considered acceptable. Political and economic pressure: here I am thinking about our Sister and Mother Earth, our planet, and about whether we are free from political and economic pressure and able to protect her, to prevent her from self-destruction. We have two conferences ahead of us, in Peru and France, that challenge us to protect the planet. I remember a phrase that I heard from an elderly man many years ago: "God always forgives offenses and abuses; God always forgives. Men forgive at times; but the earth never forgives!" Protect our Sister Earth, our Mother Earth, so that she does not react with destruction. But, above all, no system of discrimination, *de facto* or *de jure*, linked to the ability to access the market of foodstuffs, must be taken as a model for international actions that aim to eliminate hunger.

By sharing these reflections with you, I ask that the Almighty, God rich in mercy, bless all those who, with different responsibilities, place themselves at the service of those who suffer from hunger and know how to assist them with concrete gestures of closeness. I also pray that the international community might hear the appeal of this conference and consider it an expression of the common conscience of humanity: to feed the hungry, in order to save life on the planet.

SPIRITUAL MOTIVATIONS FOR CARING FOR CREATION

To my Venerable Brothers

Cardinal Peter Kodwo Appiah Turkson,
President of the Pontifical Council for Justice and Peace

Cardinal Kurt Koch,
*President of the Pontifical Council for
the Promotion of Christian Unity*

Sharing[4] the concern of my beloved brother, Ecumenical Patriarch Bartholomew, for the future of creation (cf. *Laudato Si'*, 7–9), and at the suggestion of his representative, Metropolitan Ioannis of Pergamum, who took part in the presentation of the encyclical *Laudato Si',* on care for our common home, I wish to inform you that I have decided to institute in the Catholic Church the World Day of Prayer for the Care of Creation which, beginning this year, is to be celebrated on September 1, as has been the custom in the Orthodox Church for some time.

As Christians we wish to contribute to resolving the ecological crisis which humanity is presently experiencing. In doing so, we must first rediscover in our own rich spiritual patrimony the deepest motivations for our concern for the care of creation. We need always to keep in mind that, for believers in Jesus Christ, the Word of God who became man for our sake,

> the life of the spirit is not dissociated from the body or from nature or from worldly realities, but lived in and with them, in communion with all that surrounds us. (*Laudato Si'*, 216)

The ecological crisis thus summons us to a profound spiritual conversion: Christians are called to "an ecological conversion whereby the effects of their encounter with Jesus Christ become evident in their relationship with the world around them" (ibid., 217).

For

> living our vocation to be protectors of God's handiwork is essential to a life of virtue; it is not an optional or a secondary aspect of our Christian experience. (ibid.)

The annual World Day of Prayer for the Care of Creation will offer individual believers and communities a fitting opportunity to reaffirm their personal vocation to be stewards of creation, to thank God for the wonderful handiwork which he has entrusted to our care, and to implore his help for the protection of creation as well as his pardon for the sins committed against the world in which we live. The celebration of this day, on the same date as the Orthodox Church, will be a valuable opportunity to bear witness to our growing communion with our Orthodox brothers and sisters. We live at a time when all Christians are faced with the same decisive challenges, to which we must respond together in order to be more credible and effective. It is my hope that this day will in some way also involve other churches and ecclesial communities, and be celebrated in union with similar initiatives of the World Council of Churches.

I ask you, Cardinal Turkson, as president of the Pontifical Council for Justice and Peace, to inform the Justice and Peace Commissions of the bishops' conferences, as well as the national and international organizations involved in environmental issues, of the establishment of the World Day of Prayer for the Care of Creation, so that, with due regard for local needs and situations, it can be properly celebrated with the participation of the entire People of God: priests, men and women religious, and the lay faithful. For this reason, it will be the task of your council, in cooperation with the various episcopal conferences, to arrange suitable ways of publicizing and celebrating the day, so that this annual event will become a significant occasion for prayer, reflection, conversion, and the adoption of appropriate lifestyles.

I ask you, Cardinal Koch, as president of the Pontifical Council for the Promotion of Christian Unity, to make the necessary contacts with the ecumenical patriarchate and with other ecumenical organizations so that this World Day can serve as a sign of a common journey in which all believers in Christ take part. It will also be your council's responsibility to ensure that it is coordinated with similar initiatives undertaken by the World Council of Churches.

In expressing my hope that, as a result of wide cooperation, the World Day of Prayer for the Care of Creation will be inaugurated and develop in the best way possible, I invoke upon this initiative the intercession of Mary, Mother of God, and of Saint Francis of Assisi, whose *Canticle of the Creatures* inspires so many men and women of goodwill to live in praise of the Creator and with respect for creation.

LET US PRACTICE MERCY TOWARD OUR COMMON HOME

United[5] with our Orthodox brothers and sisters, and with the support of other churches and Christian communities, the Catholic Church today marks the World Day of Prayer for the Care of Creation. This day offers

> individual believers and communities a fitting opportunity to reaffirm their personal vocation to be stewards of creation, to thank God for the wonderful handiwork which he has entrusted to our care, and to implore his help for the protection of creation as

well as his pardon for the sins committed against the world in which we live.[6]

It is most encouraging that concern for the future of our planet is shared by the churches and Christian communities, together with other religions. Indeed, in past decades numerous efforts have been made by religious leaders and organizations to call public attention to the dangers of an irresponsible exploitation of our planet. Here I would mention Patriarch Bartholomew of Constantinople who, like his predecessor Patriarch Dimitrios, has long spoken out against the sin of harming creation and has drawn attention to the moral and spiritual crisis at the root of environmental problems. In response to a growing concern for the integrity of creation, the Third European Ecumenical Assembly in Sibiu in 2007 proposed celebrating a "Time for Creation" during the five weeks between September 1 (the Orthodox commemoration of God's creation) and October 4 (the commemoration of Francis of Assisi in the Catholic Church and some other Western traditions). This initiative, supported by the World Council of Churches, has since inspired many ecumenical activities in different parts of the world. It is also encouraging that throughout the world similar initiatives promoting environmental justice, concern for the poor, and responsible social commitment have been bringing together people, especially young people, from diverse religious backgrounds. Christians or not, as people of faith and goodwill, we should be united in showing mercy to the earth as our common home and cherishing the world in which we live as a place for sharing and communion.

The earth cries out ...

With this message, I renew my dialogue with every person living on this planet about the sufferings of the poor and the devastation of the environment. God gave us a bountiful garden, but we have turned it into a polluted wasteland of "debris, desolation, and filth" (*Laudato Si'*, 161). We must not be indifferent or resigned to the loss of biodiversity and the destruction of ecosystems, often caused by our irresponsible and selfish behavior.

> Because of us, thousands of species will no longer give glory to God by their very existence, nor convey their message to us. We have no such right. (ibid., 33)

Global warming continues, due in part to human activity: 2015 was the warmest year on record, and 2016 will likely be warmer still. This is leading to ever more severe droughts, floods, fires, and extreme weather events. Climate change is also contributing to the heart-rending refugee crisis. The world's poor, though least responsible for climate change, are most vulnerable and already suffering its impact.

As an integral ecology emphasizes, human beings are deeply connected with all of creation. When we mistreat nature, we also mistreat human beings. At the same time, each creature has its own intrinsic value that must be respected. Let us hear "both the cry of the earth and the cry of the poor" (ibid., 49) and do our best to ensure an appropriate and timely response.

... for we have sinned

God gave us the earth "to till and to keep" (Gn 2:15) in a balanced and respectful way. To till too much, to keep too little, is to sin. My brother Ecumenical Patriarch Bartholomew has courageously and prophetically continued to point out our sins against creation.

> For human beings ... to destroy the biological diversity of God's creation; for human beings to degrade the integrity of the earth by causing changes in its climate, by stripping the earth of its natural forests or destroying its wetlands; for human beings to contaminate the earth's waters, its land, its air, and its life — these are sins. ... To commit a crime against the natural world is a sin against ourselves and a sin against God.[7]

In the light of what is happening to our common home, may the present Jubilee of Mercy summon the Christian faithful "to profound interior conversion" (*Laudato Si'*, 217), sustained particularly by the Sacrament of Penance. During this Jubilee Year, let us learn to implore God's mercy for those sins against creation that we have not hitherto acknowledged and confessed. Let us likewise commit ourselves to taking concrete steps toward ecological conversion, which requires a clear recognition of our responsibility to ourselves, our neighbors, creation, and the Creator (ibid., 10, 229).

An examination of conscience and repentance

The first step in this process is always an examination of conscience, which involves

> gratitude and gratuitousness, a recognition that the
> world is God's loving gift, and that we are called
> quietly to imitate his generosity in self-sacrifice and
> good works. ... It also entails a loving awareness that
> we are not disconnected from the rest of creatures,
> but joined in a splendid universal communion. As
> believers, we do not look at the world from without
> but from within, conscious of the bonds with which
> the Father has linked us to all beings. (ibid., 220)

Turning to this bountiful and merciful Father who awaits
the return of each of his children, we can acknowledge our
sins against creation, the poor, and future generations. "In-
asmuch as we all generate small ecological damage," we are
called to acknowledge "our contribution, smaller or greater,
to the disfigurement and destruction of creation."[8] This is the
first step on the path of conversion.

In 2000, also a Jubilee Year, my predecessor Saint John
Paul II asked Catholics to make amends for past and present religious intolerance, as well as for injustice toward Jews,
women, indigenous peoples, immigrants, the poor, and the
unborn. In this Extraordinary Jubilee of Mercy, I invite everyone to do likewise. As individuals, we have grown com-
fortable with certain lifestyles shaped by a distorted culture
of prosperity and a "disordered desire to consume more than
what is really necessary" (ibid., 123), and we are participants
in a system that "has imposed the mentality of profit at any
price, with no concern for social exclusion or the destruction

of nature."[9] Let us repent of the harm we are doing to our common home.

After a serious examination of conscience and moved by sincere repentance, we can confess our sins against the Creator, against creation, and against our brothers and sisters. "The Catechism of the Catholic Church presents the confessional as the place where the truth makes us free."[10] We know that "God is greater than our sin,"[11] than all our sins, including those against the environment. We confess them because we are penitent and desire to change. The merciful grace of God received in the sacrament will help us to do so.

Changing course

Examining our consciences, repentance, and confession to our Father, who is rich in mercy, lead to *a firm purpose of amendment*. This in turn must translate into concrete ways of thinking and acting that are more respectful of creation — for example, "avoiding the use of plastic and paper, reducing water consumption, separating refuse, cooking only what can reasonably be consumed, showing care for other living beings, using public transport or car-pooling, planting trees, turning off unnecessary lights, or any number of other practices" (*Laudato Si'*, 211). We must not think that these efforts are too small to improve our world. They "call forth a goodness which, albeit unseen, inevitably tends to spread" and encourage "a prophetic and contemplative lifestyle, one capable of deep enjoyment free of the obsession with consumption" (ibid., 212, 222).

In the same way, the resolve to live differently should affect our various contributions to shaping the culture and society in which we live. Indeed, "care for nature is part of a lifestyle which includes the capacity for living together and communion" (ibid., 228). Economics and politics, society and culture cannot be dominated by thinking only of the short-term and immediate financial or electoral gains. Instead, they urgently need to be redirected to the common good, which includes sustainability and care for creation.

One concrete case is the "ecological debt" between the global north and south (cf. ibid., 51–52). Repaying it would require treating the environments of poorer nations with care and providing the financial resources and technical assistance needed to help them deal with climate change and promote sustainable development.

The protection of our common home requires a growing global political consensus. Along these lines, I am gratified that in September 2015 the nations of the world adopted the Sustainable Development Goals, and that, in December 2015, they approved the Paris Agreement on climate change, which set the demanding yet fundamental goal of halting the rise of the global temperature. Now governments are obliged to honor the commitments they made, while businesses must also responsibly do their part. It is up to citizens to insist that this happen, and indeed to advocate for even more ambitious goals.

Changing course thus means "keeping the original commandment to preserve creation from all harm, both for our sake and for the sake of our fellow human beings."[12] A single question can keep our eyes fixed on the goal: "What kind of world do we want to leave to those who come after us, to children who are now growing up?" (*Laudato Si'*, 160).

A new work of mercy

Nothing unites us to God more than an act of mercy, for it is by mercy that the Lord forgives our sins and gives us the grace to practice acts of mercy in his name.[13]

To paraphrase Saint James,

We can say that mercy without works is dead. ... In our rapidly changing and increasingly globalized world, many new forms of poverty are appearing. In response to them, we need to be creative in developing new and practical forms of charitable outreach as concrete expressions of the way of mercy.[14]

The Christian life involves the practice of the traditional seven corporal and seven spiritual works of mercy.[15]

We usually think of the works of mercy individually and in relation to a specific initiative: hospitals for the sick, soup kitchens for the hungry, shelters for the homeless, schools for those to be educated, the confessional and spiritual direction for those needing counsel and forgiveness. ... But if we look at the works of mercy as a whole, we see that the object of mercy is human life itself and everything it embraces.[16]

Obviously "human life itself and everything it embraces" includes care for our common home. So let me propose a complement to the two traditional sets of seven: may the works of mercy also include *care for our common home.*

As a spiritual work of mercy, care for our common home calls for a "grateful contemplation of God's world" (*Laudato Si'*, 214) which "allows us to discover in each thing a teaching which God wishes to hand on to us" (ibid., 85). As a corporal work of mercy, care for our common home requires simple daily gestures which break with the logic of violence, exploitation and selfishness ... makes itself felt in every action that seeks to build a better world (ibid., 230, 231).

In conclusion, let us pray

Despite our sins and the daunting challenges before us, we never lose heart.

> The Creator does not abandon us; he never forsakes his loving plan or repents of having created us ... for he has united himself definitively to our earth, and his love constantly impels us to find new ways forward. (*Laudato Si'*, 13, 245)

In a particular way, let us pray on September 1, and indeed throughout the year:

> "O God of the poor,
> help us to rescue the abandoned
> and forgotten of this earth,
> who are so precious in your eyes ...
> God of love, show us our place in this world
> as channels of your love

for all the creatures of this earth" (ibid., 246),
God of mercy, may we receive your forgiveness
and convey your mercy throughout our common
home.
Praise be to you!
Amen.

PERSONAL, SOCIAL, AND ECOLOGICAL CONVERSION

Dear brothers and sisters of Brazil!

I wish[17] to join you in the Fraternity Campaign which, in this year 2017, has as its theme "Fraternity: Brazilian Ecosystems and the Defense of Life," encouraging you to spread the awareness that the global challenge, which all humanity faces, requires the dedication of each person together with implementation by each local community, as I pointed out in several points of the encyclical *Laudato Si'*, about the care of our common home.

The Creator has been bounteous to Brazil. He granted it a diversity of ecosystems that give it extraordinary beauty.

Unfortunately, however, there are also signs of aggression to creation and degradation of nature. Among you the Church has been a prophetic voice in respect and care for the environment and the poor. Not only has she drawn attention to ecological challenges and problems, but she has pointed out their causes, and above all has indicated ways to overcome them. Among the many initiatives and actions, I like to recall that already in 1979 the Fraternity Campaign, whose theme was "For a More Human World," chose the motto "Preserving What Belongs to All." Thus the Brazilian Episcopal Conference already that year expressed to Brazilian society its concern for environmental issues and human behavior toward the gifts of creation.

The objective of this year's Fraternity Campaign, inspired by a passage from the Book of Genesis (cf. 2:15), is to preserve creation, especially the Brazilian ecosystems, God's gifts, and to promote fraternal relationships with the life and culture of peoples in the light of the Gospel. Since "we cannot fail to consider the effects on people's lives of environmental deterioration, current models of development and the throwaway culture" (*Laudato Si'*, 43), this campaign invites us to contemplate, admire, be grateful for, and respect the natural diversity which is manifested in the different ecosystems of Brazil — a true gift of God — through the promotion of relationships which respect the life and culture of the peoples who live in them. This is exactly one of the greatest challenges in every part of the world, not least because the degradation of the environment is always accompanied by social injustice.

The original peoples of each ecosystem, or those who

traditionally live in it, offer us a clear example of how living together with creation can be respectful, bearing fullness and mercy. Therefore it is necessary to know and learn from these peoples and their relationship with nature. In this way it will be possible to find a model of sustainability that can be an alternative to the unbridled desire for profit that depletes natural resources and wounds the dignity of the poor.

Every year the Fraternity Campaign takes place in the intense period of Lent. It is an invitation to live Paschal spirituality with greater awareness and determination. The communion in the Pasch of Jesus Christ is capable of inspiring a permanent and integral conversion that is at once personal, communitarian, social, and ecological. I therefore repeat what I recalled on the occasion of the extraordinary Holy Year: mercy demands restoring "dignity to all those from whom it has been robbed" (*Misericordiae Vultus*, 16). A person of faith who celebrates the victory of life over death at Easter cannot remain indifferent upon realizing the situation of aggression against God's creation in each of the Brazilian ecosystems.

I wish everyone a fruitful Lenten journey and I pray to God that the 2017 Fraternity Campaign will achieve its goals. In invoking the companionship and protection of *Nossa Senhora Aparecida* (Our Lady of Aparecida) on all the Brazilian people, especially in this Marian year, I impart a special apostolic blessing and ask you to never stop praying for me.

THE RIGHT TO WATER

I greet[18] all of you present here and thank you for your participation in this meeting that addresses the issue of the human right to water and the need for public policies to deal with this reality. It is significant that you are coming together to bring your knowledge and resources to bear in order to respond to this need and to this problem that people live today.

As we read in the Book of Genesis, water is at the beginning of all things (cf. 1:2); it is "a useful, pure, and humble creature," the source of life and fruitfulness (cf. Francis of Assisi, *Canticle of the Creatures*). Therefore the question you are dealing with is not peripheral, but fundamental and very urgent. Fundamental because where there is water there is life, and society can then rise and progress. And it is urgent because our common home needs protection and, moreover, we understand that not all water is life: only water that is safe and of good quality. Remaining with the figure of Saint Francis, it is only water that "serves with humility," water that is "chaste," not polluted.

Each and every person has the right to access safe drinking water. It is an essential human right and one of the crucial issues in today's world (cf. *Laudato Si'*, 30; *Caritas in Veritate,* 27). It is painful when the legislation of a country or group of countries does not consider water as a human right. And it is even more painful when what was written is neglected and this human right is denied. It is a problem that concerns everyone, makes our common home bear so much misery, and cries out for effective solutions, truly capable of overcoming the selfishness that prevents the implementation of this vital right for all human beings. It is necessary to give water the centrality it deserves in public policy. Our right to water is also a duty toward water. From the right we have to it comes an obligation that binds us to it and cannot be sundered. It is vital to proclaim this essential human right and defend it — as we are doing — but also to act in a concrete way, ensuring a political and legal commitment to water. In this sense, each state is called to concretize, including by juridical means, what is indicated by the resolutions approved by the General Assembly of the United Nations in 2010 on the Human Right to Drinking Water and Sanitation. On the other hand, every non-state actor must assume its responsibilities toward this right.

The right to water is decisive for people's survival (cf. *Laudato Si'*, 30) and decides the future of humanity. It is also a priority to educate the next generations about the gravity of this reality. The formation of conscience is a difficult task; it requires conviction and dedication. I wonder if, in the midst of this "piecemeal third world war" we are experiencing, we are not going toward the great world war over water.

The figures revealed by the United Nations are shocking and cannot leave us indifferent: a thousand children die every day from water-related diseases. Millions of people consume polluted water. These figures are very serious; this situation must be curbed and reversed. It is not too late, but it is urgent to become aware of the need for water and its essential value for the good of humanity.

Respect for water is a condition for the exercise of other human rights (ibid., 30). If we respect this right as fundamental, we lay the foundations to protect other rights. But if we violate this essential right, how can we watch over others and fight for them? In this commitment to give water its rightful place, a culture of care is needed (ibid., 231) — it seems poetic, and indeed creation is a "poiesis," this culture of care that is creative — and also to promote a culture of encounter, in which all the necessary forces of scientists and business people, rulers, and politicians unite in a common cause. It is necessary to unite all our voices in the same cause. They will no longer be individual or isolated voices, but the cry of the brother who cries out through us is the cry of the earth calling for respect and responsible sharing of a good that belongs to all. In this culture of encounter, the action of each state as guarantor of universal access to safe and good quality water is indispensable.

God the Creator does not abandon us in this labor to

give each and every person access to safe drinking water. But the work is ours, the responsibility is ours. I hope that this seminar will be a good opportunity for you to see your convictions strengthened and leave here with the certainty that your work is necessary and a priority for other people to live. It is an ideal for which it is worth fighting and working. With our "little" we will help to make our common home more habitable and more united, more cared for, a home where no one is discarded or excluded, but where we all enjoy the goods necessary to live and grow in dignity. And let us not forget the data, the figures of the United Nations. Let us not forget that every day a thousand children die from water-related diseases — every day!

NEW LIFESTYLES

The[19] story of creation presents us with a panoramic view of the world. Scripture reveals that "in the beginning" God intended humanity to cooperate in the preservation and protection of the natural environment. At first, as we read in Genesis,

> no plant of the field was yet in the earth and no herb of the field had yet sprung up — for the Lord God had not caused it to rain upon the earth, and there was no one to till the ground. (2:5)

The earth was entrusted to us as a sublime gift and legacy, for which all of us share responsibility until, "in the end," all things in heaven and on earth will be restored in Christ (cf. Eph 1:10). Our human dignity and welfare are deeply connected to our care for the whole of creation.

However, "in the meantime," the history of the world presents a very different context. It reveals a morally decaying scenario where our attitude and behavior toward creation obscures our calling as God's cooperators. Our propensity to interrupt the world's delicate and balanced ecosystems, our insatiable desire to manipulate and control the planet's limited resources, and our greed for limitless profit in markets — all these have alienated us from the original purpose of creation. We no longer respect nature as a shared gift; instead, we regard it as a private possession. We no longer associate with nature in order to sustain it; instead, we lord over it to support our own constructs.

The consequences of this alternative worldview are tragic and lasting. The human environment and the natural environment are deteriorating together, and this deterioration of the planet weighs upon the most vulnerable of its people. The impact of climate change affects, first and foremost, those who live in poverty in every corner of the globe. Our obligation to use the earth's goods responsibly implies the recognition of and respect for all people and all living creatures. The urgent call and challenge to care for creation are an invitation for all of humanity to work toward sustainable and integral development.

Therefore, united by the same concern for God's creation and acknowledging the earth as a shared good, we fervently invite all people of goodwill to dedicate a time of prayer for the environment on September 1. On this occasion, we wish to offer thanks to the loving Creator for the noble gift of creation and to pledge commitment to its care and preservation for the sake of future generations. After all, we know that we labor in vain if the Lord is not by our side (cf. Ps 126–127), if prayer is not at the center of our reflection and celebration. Indeed, an objective of our prayer is to change the way we perceive the world in order to change the way we relate to the world. The goal of our promise is to be courageous in embracing greater simplicity and solidarity in our lives.

We urgently appeal to those in positions of social and economic, as well as political and cultural**,** responsibility to hear the cry of the earth and to attend to the needs of the marginalized, but above all to respond to the plea of millions and support the consensus of the world for the healing of our wounded creation. We are convinced that there can be no sincere and enduring resolution to the challenge of the ecological crisis and climate change unless the response is concerted and collective, unless the responsibility is shared and accountable, unless we give priority to solidarity and service.

LIFE-GIVING WATER

On[20] this day of prayer, I wish first to thank the Lord for the gift of our common home and for all those men and women of goodwill committed to protecting it. I am likewise grateful for the many projects aimed at promoting the study and the safeguarding of ecosystems, for the efforts being made to develop more sustainable agriculture and more responsible nutrition, and for the various educational, spiritual, and liturgical initiatives that involve Christians throughout the world in the care of creation.

It must be acknowledged that we have not succeeded in responsibly protecting creation. The environmental situation, both on the global level and in many specific places, cannot be considered satisfactory. Rightly, there is a growing sense of the need for a renewed and sound relationship between humanity and creation, and the conviction that only an authentic and integral vision of humanity will permit us to take better care of our planet for the benefit of present and future generations. For "there is no ecology without an adequate anthropology" (*Laudato Si'*, 118).

On this World Day of Prayer for the Care of Creation, which the Catholic Church for several years now has celebrated in union with our Orthodox brothers and sisters and with participation of other churches and Christian communities, I would like to draw attention to the question of *water*. It is a very simple and precious element, yet access to it is, sadly, for many people difficult if not impossible. Nonetheless,

> access to safe drinkable water is a basic and universal human right, since it is essential to human survival and, as such, is a condition for the exercise of other human rights. Our world owes a great social debt toward the poor who lack access to drinking water, because they are denied the right to a life consistent with their inalienable dignity. (*Laudato Si'*, 30)

Water invites us to reflect on our origins. The human body is mostly composed of water, and many civilizations throughout history arose near great rivers that marked their identity. In an evocative image, the beginning of the Book of Genesis states that, in the beginning, the spirit of the Creator "swept over the face of the waters" (1:2).

In considering the fundamental role of water in creation and in human development, I feel the need to give thanks to God for "Sister Water," simple and useful for life like nothing else on our planet. Precisely for this reason, care for water sources and water basins is an urgent imperative. Today, more than ever, we need to look beyond immediate concerns (cf. *Laudato Si'*, 36) and beyond a purely utilitarian view of reality "in which efficiency and productivity are entirely geared to our individual benefit" (ibid., 159). We urgently need shared projects and concrete gestures that recognize that every privatization of the natural good of water, at the expense of the human right to have access to this good, is unacceptable.

For us Christians, water represents an essential element of purification and of life. We think immediately of baptism, the sacrament of our rebirth. Water made holy by the Spirit is the matter by which God has given us life and renewed us; it is the blessed source of undying life. For Christians of different confessions, baptism also represents the real and irreplaceable point of departure for experiencing an ever more authentic fraternity on the way to full unity. Jesus, in the course of his mission, promised a water capable of quenching human thirst forever (cf. Jn 4:14). He prophesied, "If any one thirst, let him come to me and drink" (Jn 7:37). To drink from Jesus means to encounter him personally as the Lord, drawing from his words the meaning of life. May the words he spoke from the cross — "I thirst" (Jn 19:28) — echo constantly in our hearts. The Lord continues to ask that his thirst be quenched; he thirsts for love. He asks us to give him to drink in all those who thirst in our own day, and to say to them, "I was thirsty and you gave me to drink" (Mt 25:35). To give to drink, in the global village, does not only entail personal gestures of charity, but also concrete choices and a constant commitment to ensure to all the primary good of water.

I would like also to mention the issue of the seas and oceans. It is our duty to thank the Creator for the impressive and marvelous gift of the great waters and all that they contain (cf. Gn 1:20–21; Ps 146:6), and to praise him for covering the earth with the oceans (cf. Ps 104:6). To ponder the immense open seas and their incessant movement can also represent an opportunity to turn our thoughts to God, who constantly accompanies his creation, guiding its course and sustaining its existence.[21]

Constant care for this inestimable treasure represents today an ineluctable duty and a genuine challenge. There is need for an effective cooperation between men and women of goodwill in assisting the ongoing work of the Creator. Sadly, all too many efforts fail due to the lack of effective regulation and means of control, particularly with regard to the protection of marine areas beyond national confines (cf. *Laudato Si'*, 174). We cannot allow our seas and oceans to be littered by endless fields of floating plastic. Here, too, our active commitment is needed to confront this emergency. We need to pray as if everything depended on God's providence, and work as if everything depended on us.

Let us pray that waters may not be a sign of separation between peoples, but of encounter for the human community. Let us pray that those who risk their lives at sea in search of a better future may be kept safe. Let us ask the Lord and all those engaged in the noble service of politics that the more sensitive questions of our day, such as those linked to movements of migration, climate change, and the right of everyone to enjoy primary goods may be faced with generous and farsighted responsibility and a spirit of cooperation, especially among those countries most able to help.

Let us pray, too, for all those who devote themselves to the apostolate of the sea, for those who help reflect on the issues involving maritime ecosystems, for those who contribute to the development and application of international regulations on the seas in order to safeguard individuals, countries, goods, natural resources — I think, for example, of marine fauna and flora, and coral reefs (cf. ibid., 41) or seabeds — and to guarantee an integral development in view of the common good of the entire human family and not particular interests. Let us remember, too, all those who work to protect maritime areas and to safeguard the oceans and their biodiversity, that they may carry out this task with responsibility and integrity.

Finally, let us be concerned for the younger generation and pray for them, that they may grow in knowledge and respect for our common home and in the desire to care for the essential good of water, for the benefit of all. It is my prayerful hope that Christian communities may contribute more and more concretely helping everyone to enjoy this indispensable resource, in respectful care for the gifts received from the Creator, and in particular rivers, seas, and oceans.

THE EARTH MUST BE TREATED WITH TENDERNESS

I[22] am grateful that you have invited me to address you at the beginning of the conference "Water, Agriculture and Food: Let Us Build Tomorrow," organized by various academic, social, and ecclesial institutions, with the participation of the United Nations Food and Agriculture Organizations based in Rome.

The theme that has brought them together reminds me of the psalmist, who gratefully acknowledges that "The Lord will indeed give what is good, / and our land will yield its harvest" (Ps 85:12). In another moment, the prophet Isaiah compares the word of God with the rainwater that soaks the earth, making it germinate "so that it yields seed for the sower / and bread for the eater" (Is 55:10). The rain, the harvest, the food. Biblical wisdom saw a close link between these elements and interpreted them from the perspective of gratitude, never from voracity or exploitation. The faith and experience of believers leads to this recognition, which transforms for us into a pressing call to responsibility, not to be caught in petty calculations that prevent us from helping the less favored, who are deprived of their most basic needs. In this regard, the subtitle that they wanted to give their thoughts is inspiring, because the word "build" implies a sense of positivity, the contribution of a benefit, openness to the other, reciprocity, and collaboration. These key words must not be forgotten, because the tomorrow we all want can only be the result of loyal, supportive, and generous cooperation.

Indeed, the challenges to humanity at the present time are so complex that they require a sum of ideas, a unity of efforts, a complementarity of perspectives, while renouncing exclusionary selfishness and pernicious protagonism. In this way, sound decisions will be taken and solid foundations can be laid to build a fair and inclusive society in which no one is left behind. A society that puts the human being and his fundamental rights at the center, without being led astray by questionable interests that only enrich a few, unfortunately always the same. This will also be the way to ensure that future generations find a harmonious world without quarrels, with the necessary resources to enjoy a dignified and full life.

Although the land has resources for everyone, in terms of both quantity and quality, a large number of people suffer from hunger and are cruelly afflicted by poverty. To eradicate these scourges, it would be enough to eliminate injustices and inequities and put in place farsighted and far-reaching policies, effective and coordinated measures, so that no one may lack daily bread or the means necessary to exist. Among them, water is essential and yet, unfortunately, not everyone has access to it, so it is essential that it be better distributed and managed in a sustainable and rational manner. Likewise it is also unavoidable to ensure the care and protection of the environment, safeguarding its beauty, preserving the copious variety of ecosystems, cultivating the fields with care, without greed and without causing irreversible damage.

The earth must be treated with tenderness, so as not to cause it damage, so as not to ruin the work of the hands of the Creator. When this is not done, the earth ceases to be a source of life for the human family. And this is what happens in many regions of our planet, where water is contaminated, garbage accumulates, deforestation advances, air is stale, and soil acidified. All this generates a harmful accumulation of ills and miseries, which we also find when food is wasted and not shared; that is why it is essential to educate children and young people to nourish themselves healthily, not simply to eat. Correct nourishment involves knowing the value of food, disengagement from frenzied and compulsive consumerism, and making the table a place for encounter and fraternity, not just the space for ostentation, waste, or whims.

I ask God the Father that all those who participate in this important day leave it with a renewed desire to make the earth the common home that welcomes us all, a home of open doors, a place of communion and beneficial coexistence. In this way, the future will be full of light and can be faced by all with confidence and hope, as the fruit of a serene present rich in seeds of virtue and hope.

FAITH, INCLUSION, AND SUSTAINABLE DEVELOPMENT

Sustainability and Inclusion

When[23] we speak of sustainability, we cannot overlook how important it is to include and to listen to all voices, especially those usually excluded from this type of discussion, such as the voices of the poor, migrants, indigenous people, the young. I am pleased to see a variety of participants at this conference bringing a wide range of voices, of opinions and proposals, which can contribute to new paths of constructive development. It is important that the implementation of the sustainable development goals truly respect their original nature, which is inclusive and participatory.

The 2030 Agenda and the Sustainable Development Goals, approved by more than 190 nations in September 2015, were a great step forward for global dialogue, marking a vitally "new and universal solidarity" (*Laudato Si'*, 14). Different religious traditions, including the Catholic tradition, have embraced the objectives of sustainable development because they are the result of global participatory processes that, on the one hand, reflect the values of people and, on the other, are sustained by an integral vision of development.

Integral Development

Nevertheless, proposing a dialogue on inclusive and sustainable development also requires acknowledging that "development" is a complex concept, which is often manipulated. When we speak of development, we must always ask: Development of what? Development for whom? For too long the conventional idea of development has been almost entirely limited to economic growth. Indicators of national development have been based on gross domestic product (GDP) indices. This has led the modern economic system down a dangerous path where progress is assessed only in terms of material growth, on account of which we are almost obliged to irrationally exploit the environment and our fellow human beings.

As my predecessor Saint Paul VI rightly highlighted, to speak about human development means referring to *all* people — not just a few — and to the *whole* person — not just the material dimension (cf. *Populorum Progressio*, 14). Any fruitful discussion of development, therefore, should offer viable models of social integration and ecological conversion, because we cannot develop ourselves as human beings by fomenting increased inequality and degradation of the environment.[24]

Rejecting negative models, and proposing alternative ways forward, applies not only to others, but also to us. We should all commit ourselves to promoting and implementing the development goals that are supported by our deepest religious and ethical values. Human development is not only an economic issue or one that concerns experts alone; it is ultimately a vocation, a call that requires a free and responsible answer (cf. Benedict XVI, *Caritas in Veritate*, 16–17).

Goals (Dialogue and Commitments)

Solutions are what I hope will emerge from this conference: Concrete responses to the cry of the earth and the cry of the poor. Concrete commitments to promoting real development in a sustainable way through processes open to people's participation. Concrete proposals to facilitate the development of those in need, making use of what Pope Benedict XVI recognized as "the unprecedented possibility of large-scale redistribution of wealth on a worldwide scale" (ibid., 42). Concrete economic policies that are focused on the person and that can promote a more humane market and society (cf. ibid., 45–47). Concrete economic measures that seriously take into consideration our common home. Concrete ethical, civil, and political commitments that develop *alongside* our Sister Earth, and never *against* her.

Everything Is Connected

I am also pleased to know that the participants in this conference are willing to listen to religious voices when they discuss the implementation of the sustainable development goals. All those involved in dialogue on this complex issue are invited in some way to go beyond their areas of specialization to find a shared response to the cry of the earth and of the poor. Those of us who are religious need to open up the treasures of our best traditions in order to engage in a true and respectful dialogue on how to build the future of our planet. Religious narratives, though ancient, are usually full of symbolism and contain

> a conviction which we today share, that everything is interconnected, and that genuine care for our own lives and our relationships with nature is inseparable from fraternity, justice, and faithfulness to others. (*Laudato Si'*, 70)

In this respect, the United Nations 2030 Agenda proposes integrating all the goals through the 'five Ps': people, planet, prosperity, peace, and partnership.[25] I know that this conference is also focusing on these five Ps.

I welcome this unified approach to these goals, which can also help to save us from an understanding of prosperity that is based on the myth of unlimited growth and consumption (cf. *Laudato Si'*, 106), where we depend only on technological progress for sustainability. There are still people who stubbornly uphold this myth, and who tell us that social and ecological problems will solve themselves simply by the application of new technologies, without any need for ethical considerations or profound change (cf. ibid., 60).

An integral approach teaches us that this is not true. While it is certainly necessary to aim for a set of development goals, this is not sufficient for a fair and sustainable world order. Economic and political objectives must be sustained by ethical objectives, which presuppose a change of attitude: what the Bible would call a change of heart. Already Saint John Paul II spoke about the need to "encourage and support the 'ecological conversion'" (Catechesis, January 17, 2001). This word is powerful: *ecological conversion.* Religions have a key role to play in this. For a correct shift toward a sustainable future, we must recognize "our errors, sins, faults, and failures," which leads to a "heartfelt repentance and desire to change"; in this way, we will be reconciled with others, with creation, and with the Creator (cf. *Laudato Si'*, 218).

If we want to provide a solid foundation for the work of the 2030 Agenda, we must reject the temptation to look for a merely technocratic response to the challenges — this is not good — and be prepared to address the root causes and the long-term consequences.

Indigenous Peoples

The key principle of all religions is the love of neighbor and the care of creation. I wish to draw attention to a special group of religious persons — namely, indigenous peoples. Although they represent only 5 percent of the world's population, they look after about 22 percent of the earth's landmass. Living in areas such as the Amazon and the Arctic, they help protect approximately 80 percent of the planet's biodiversity. According to UNESCO:

> Indigenous peoples are custodians and practitioners of unique cultures and relationships with the natural environment. They embody a wide range of linguistic and cultural diversity at the heart of our shared humanity.[26]

I would also add that, in a strongly secularized world, such peoples remind us all of the sacredness of our earth. This means that their voice and their concerns should be at the center of the implementation of the 2030 Agenda and at the heart of the search for new paths for a sustainable future. I will also be discussing this with my brother bishops at the Synod for the Pan-Amazon Region, at the end of October this year.

Conclusions

Dear brothers and sisters, today, after three and a half years since the adoption of the sustainable development goals, we must be even more acutely aware of the importance of accelerating and adapting our actions in responding adequately to both the cry of the earth and the cry of the poor (cf. *Laudato Si'*, 49) — they are connected.

The challenges are complex and have multiple causes; the response, therefore, must necessarily be complex and well-structured, respectful of the diverse cultural riches of peoples. If we are truly concerned about developing an ecology capable of repairing the damage we have done, no branch of science or form of wisdom should be overlooked, and this includes religions and the languages particular to them (cf. ibid., 63). Religions can help us along the path of authentic integral development, which is the new name of peace (cf. Paul VI, *Populorum Progressio*, 76–77).

I express my heartfelt appreciation for your efforts in caring for our common home at the service of promoting an inclusive sustainable future. I know that, at times, it can seem far too difficult a task. And yet, "human beings, while capable of the worst, are also capable of rising above themselves, choosing again what is good, and making a new start" (*Laudato Si'*, 205). This is the change which present circumstances demand, because the injustice that brings tears to our world and to its poor is not invincible. Thank you.

CARING FOR OUR COMMON HOME IS AN ECUMENICAL CHALLENGE

In my encyclical letter[27] *Laudato Si'*, concerned about the worrying of the planet, I underlined how important it is "to enter into dialogue with all people about our common home" (3). We need a dialogue that responds effectively to the "cry of the Earth and the cry of the poor" (ibid., 49). I am particularly appreciative that in your meeting, representatives of communities affected by mining activities and leaders of mining companies have come together around the same table. It is laudable; and it is an essential step on the way forward. We should encourage this dialogue to continue and become the norm, rather than the exception. I congratulate you for embarking on the path of mutual dialogue in the spirit of honesty, courage, and fraternity.

The precarious condition of our common home has been the result largely of a fallacious economic model that has been followed for too long. It is a voracious model, profit-oriented, shortsighted, and based on the misconception of unlimited economic growth. Although we frequently see its disastrous impacts on the natural world and in the lives of people, we are still resistant to change:

> Economic powers continue to justify the current global system where priority tends to be given to ... the pursuit of financial gain, which fail to take the context into account, let alone the effects on human dignity and the natural environment. (ibid., 56)

We are aware that

> by itself the market cannot guarantee integral human development and social inclusion (ibid., 109) [and that] environmental protection cannot be assured solely on the basis of financial calculations of costs and benefits. (ibid., 190)

We need a paradigm shift in all our economic activities, including mining.

In this context, the title for your meeting, "Mining for the Common Good," is very appropriate. What does it concretely imply? Please allow me to articulate a few reflections in this regard which could assist you in your dialogue.

First of all, mining, like all economic activities, should be at the service of the entire human community. As Pope Paul VI wrote:

> God intended the Earth and everything in it for the use of all human beings and peoples. ... Created goods should flow fairly to all. (*Populorum progressio*, 22)

It is an essential pillar of the Church's social teaching. In this perspective, the involvement of local communities is important in every phase of mining projects:

> A consensus should always be reached between the different stakeholders, who can offer a variety of approaches, solutions, and alternatives. The local population should have a special place at the table; they are concerned about their own future and that of their children, and can consider goals transcending immediate economic interest. (*Laudato Si'*, 183)

In the light of the upcoming Synod on the Amazon, I would like to stress that

> it is essential to show special care for indigenous communities and their cultural traditions. They are not merely one minority among others, but should be the principal dialogue partners, especially when large projects affecting their land are proposed. (ibid., 146)

These vulnerable communities have a lot to teach us:

> For them, land is not a commodity but rather a gift
> from God and from their ancestors who rest there, a
> sacred space with which they need to interact if they
> are to maintain their identity and values. ... Nev-
> ertheless, in various parts of the world, pressure is
> being put on them to abandon their homelands to
> make room for ... mining projects which are under-
> taken without regard for the degradation of nature
> and culture. (ibid.)

I urge everyone to respect the fundamental human rights
and voice of the persons in these beautiful yet fragile communities. Second, mining should be at the service of the human person and not vice versa. As Pope Benedict XVI wrote:

> In development programs, the principle of the cen-
> trality of the human person, as the subject primari-
> ly responsible for development, must be preserved.
> (*Caritas in Veritate*, 47)

Each and every person is precious before God's eyes, and
his or her fundamental human rights are sacred and inalienable, irrespective of one's social or economic status. Attention for the safety and well-being of the people involved in
mining operations as well as the respect for fundamental
human rights of the members of local communities and
those who champion their causes are indeed nonnegotiable
principles. Mere corporate social responsibility is not suffi-

cient. We need to ensure that mining activities lead to the integral human development of each and every person and of the entire community.

Third, we need to encourage the implementation of a circular economy, all the more in the sphere of mining activities. I find the observation that my brother bishops of Latin America made in their recent pastoral letter regarding extractive activities very pertinent. They wrote:

> By "extractivism" we understand an unbridled tendency of the economic system to convert the goods of nature into capital. The action of "extracting" the greatest amount of materials in the shortest possible time, converting them into raw materials and inputs that industry will use, that will then be transformed into products and services that others will market, society will consume and then nature itself will receive in the form of polluting waste — that is the consumerist loop that is being generated at ever greater speed and ever greater risk.[28]

We need to denounce and move away from this throwaway culture:

> Our industrial system, at the end of its cycle of production and consumption, has not developed the capacity to absorb and reuse waste and byproducts. We have not yet managed to adopt a circular model of production capable of preserving resources for present and future generations, while limiting as

much as possible the use of nonrenewable resources, moderating their consumption, maximizing their efficient use, reusing and recycling them. (*Laudato Si'*, 22)

The promotion of a circular economy and the "reduce, reuse, recycle" approach are also very much in consonance with the Sustainable Consumption and Production Patterns promoted by the 12th Sustainable Development Goal of the United Nations. Moreover, religious traditions have always presented temperance as a key component of responsible and ethical lifestyle. Moderation is also vital to save our common home. "Blessed are the meek, for they shall inherit the earth" (Mt 5:5).

My dear brothers and sisters, our efforts and struggles to safeguard our common home are truly an ecumenical journey, challenging us to think and act as members of one common home (*oecumene*). I am particularly pleased that your meeting has brought together representatives of churches and faith communities from around the world. I also thank the leaders of the mining industry for having joined this conversation. We need to act together to heal and rebuild our common home. All of us are called to "cooperate as instruments of God for the care of creation, each according to his or her own culture, experience, involvements, and talents" (*Laudato Si'*, 14).

It is my sincere hope that your meeting be truly a moment of discernment that may lead to concrete action. I pray, as my brother bishops from Latin America wrote, that you may analyze, interpret, and discern what are appropriate or inappropriate extractive activities in the territories; then, propose, plan, and act to transform our own way of life, to influence the mining and energy policies of states and governments, and in the policies and strategies of companies dedicated to extractivism, all for the purpose of achieving the common good and a genuine human development that is integral and sustainable.[29]

Your meeting is so important as you are dealing with questions that concern the future of our common home and the future of our children and the future generations:

We need to see that what is at stake is our own dignity. Leaving an inhabitable planet to future generations is, first and foremost, up to us. The issue is one which dramatically affects us, for it has to do with the ultimate meaning of our earthly sojourn. (*Laudato Si'*, 160)

May you never lose sight of this larger picture!

A GREAT HOPE*

Holy Scripture teaches us that God created the world. The Church's liturgy then confides in us that he did this to "fill with blessings" (*Roman Missal*, Preface to Eucharistic Prayer IV) everything that came out of nothing to life.

A world created as a gift

What exists therefore carries with it an imprint, a trace, a memory — dare I say genetics — that refers back to the Father. This means that, in everything that exists, the Father gives himself, and therefore we can meet him, we can have some experience of his love, we can perceive a spark of his paternity. There is nothing so small or poor that does not carry within itself this origin, or that can lose it altogether.

_____

* This text by Pope Francis is published for the first time in this volume.

We can thus borrow the words of the author of the Book of Wisdom, who addresses God, saying:

> For you love all things that exist,
> and detest none of the things that you have made,
> for you would not have made anything if you had
> hated it.
> How would anything have endured if you had not
> willed it?
> Or how would anything not called forth by you have
> been preserved?
> You spare all things, for they are yours, O LORD, you
> who love the living. (11:24–26)

There is, therefore, a continuous, radical connection between all that exists. The world comes from a loving God who gives himself within the world and calls us to share his mode of existence. Creation, however, is not, as is often thought, simply nature and environment. We are creatures. Even time that passes is a creature. This means that there is no situation, no trial or crisis, no joy or success, in which we cannot experience the Lord, take a step toward him in order to grow in friendship with him and to be able to love, in our turn, in the same way that we are passionately loved.

To live as a gift and to reveal a presence

Everything that exists, therefore, exists in order to be able to "live" as God — that is, as a gift, as love welcomed and delivered. But creation can live this only through mankind. Only in the human being, the microcosm that condenses the universe into itself, but that lives by the breath that the personal God has directly blown on his face, can the world correspond to its secret nature as sacrament — that is, be seen as a gift.

A gift is always a personal reality: In some way it contains the one who has given it and asks the one to whom it is offered to see it in this way, as a transparent reality of the giver's face, a gift made in order to show love and to make the life of the other a communion with oneself. It is the human being's task to freely and creatively decipher the revelation of this gift. And it is also his task to grasp the world in his communion with God.

Humanity's destiny determines the world's destiny

Creation is therefore a place where we are invited to discover a presence. But this means that it is the human being's capacity for communion that conditions the state of creation. This is our great responsibility. When we are unable to decipher the presence that inhabits things, everything becomes banal and opaque. It ceases to be a means of communion and becomes an opportunity for temptation and stumbling. All this begins in the heart of each one of us and spreads through thoughts, intentions, behavior and habits, both at the level of individuals and of social groups. In order to be part of this chain that trivializes or disfigures the gift of creation is not necessary to be a criminal. It is "enough" not to recognize the gift that the other — anyone else — is, from a family member to a neighbor, from the colleague at work to the poor person I meet on the street, from my friend to the migrant looking for a job or an apartment to live in. ... What happens in the heart of man has a universal meaning and is imprinted on the world. Therefore, it is the destiny of the human being that determines the destiny of the universe.

The environmental disaster: an aspect of the crisis of our time

Precisely because everything is connected (cf. *Laudato Si'*, 42, 56) in goodness, in love, precisely for this reason every lack of love has repercussions on everything. Therefore the ecological crisis we are experiencing is above all one of the effects of this unhealthy gaze upon us, on others, on the world, on the passing of time; an unhealthy gaze that does not make us perceive everything as a gift offered to discover ourselves as beloved. It is this authentic love, which sometimes reaches us in unimaginable and unexpected ways, that asks us to reassess our lifestyles, our criteria for judgment, the values on which we base our choices. In fact, it is now well known that pollution, climate change, desertification, environmental migration, unsustainable consumption of the planet's resources, acidification of the oceans, reduction of biodiversity are all aspects inseparable from social inequity (cf. *Evangelii gaudium* 52–53, 59–60, 202), of the growing concentration of power and wealth in the hands of very few and the so-called affluent societies, of outlandish military spending, of the culture of waste and a lack of consideration for the world from the standpoint of view of the peripheries, of the lack of protection of children and minors, of vulnerable elderly people, of children yet unborn.

A cultural challenge

One of the great risks of our time when facing the serious threat to life on the planet caused by the ecological crisis is failure to read this phenomenon as an aspect of a global crisis, but instead to limit ourselves to looking for purely environmental solutions, as necessary and indispensable as they are. Now, a global crisis demands a global vision and a global approach, which first of all requires a spiritual rebirth in the noblest sense of the word. Climate change could paradoxically become an opportunity to ask fundamental questions about the mystery of creation and what it is worth living for. This could lead to a profound change of our cultural and economic models, toward growth in justice and sharing, the rediscovery of the value of each person, a pledge that those who are on the margins today can be included and those who will come tomorrow can still enjoy the beauty of our world, which is and will always be a gift offered to our freedom and responsibility.

The dominant culture — the one that we breathe through reading, meetings, entertainment, the media, etc. — is founded on possession: of things, of success, of visibility, of power. Whoever has much is worth much, is admired, appreciated, and exercises some form of power. Whereas those who have little risk losing even their face, because they disappear, they become one of those invisible people who populate our cities, one of those people we do not notice or try not to come into contact with.

Each one of us is first of all a victim of this mentality, because we are bombarded by it in many ways. Since childhood we have grown up in a world where a widespread mercantile ideology, which is the true ideology and practice of globalization, stimulates within us an individualism that becomes narcissism, greed, basic ambition, denial of the other. ... In our current situation, therefore, the just and wise attitude is above all self-awareness, rather than accusation or judgment.

We are, in fact, involved in structures of sin (as Saint John Paul II called them)[1] that produce evil, pollute the environment, hurt and humiliate the poor, promote the logic of possession and power, massively exploit natural resources, force entire populations to leave their lands, and fuel hatred, violence, and war. This is a cultural and spiritual trend that distorts our spiritual sense which, instead, by virtue of our having been created in God's image and likeness, naturally orients us to goodness, love, and service to our neighbor.

For these reasons, change cannot simply come from our own commitment or from a technological revolution. Without devaluing those things, we need to rediscover ourselves as persons — that is, men and women who recognize that they are incapable of knowing who they are without others, and who feel called to see the world around them not as a goal in itself, but as a sacrament of communion.

Starting afresh from forgiveness

In this way today's problems can become real opportunities to truly discover ourselves as one family, the human family.

As we realize that we are missing the goal, that we are prioritizing what is not essential or even what is not good and is harmful, repentance and the plea for forgiveness may arise in us. I sincerely dream of growth in awareness and sincere repentance for all of us, men and women of the twenty-first century, believers and nonbelievers alike, for our societies, for letting ourselves be carried by logics that divide, starve, isolate, and condemn. It would be beautiful if we became capable of asking forgiveness from the poor, the excluded. Then we would become capable of sincerely repenting even of the harm done to the land, the sea, the air, the animals ...

Asking and giving forgiveness are actions that are possible only in the Holy Spirit, because it is he who opens the closures of individuals. And much love is needed to set aside one's pride, to realize that you have been wrong and to have hope that new paths are truly possible. So repentance, for all of us, for our era, is a grace to be humbly implored to the Lord Jesus Christ, so that history will remember this generation of ours not for its mistakes, but for the humility and wisdom of being able to reverse the course.

A possible way forward

What I am saying may seem idealistic and not very concrete, while the paths that aim at technological innovation, reducing the use of packaging, developing energy from renewable sources, etc., appear more viable. All this is undoubtedly not only necessary, but indispensable. Yet it is not enough. Ecology is the ecology of man and of creation as a whole, not just of one part. Just as in a serious illness, medicine alone is not enough, but it is necessary to look at the sick person and understand the causes that led to the onset of the affliction, so too the crisis of our time must be tackled at its roots. The proposed path, then, consists in rethinking our future starting from relationships. The men and women of our time are so thirsty for authenticity, for a sincere reassessment of the criteria of life, for focusing again on what has value, redeveloping existence, and culture.

Learning from the liturgy

Beyond personal and community commitment to the conversion of our mentality (even before behavior), a contribution we can offer as believers is precisely that of vision. And we can learn this vision day after day from the liturgy, which is the daily experience of finding ourselves in the presence of the risen and victorious Lord, to share with him in the salvation of creation as a whole.

This is particularly evident in the Mass, which is the thanksgiving to God par excellence. In it we offer to the Father what comes from him (the wheat and grapes) transformed by the wise work of human beings into our food, our drink — that is those elements on which we feed in order to live, and live to the best of our ability. On the one hand, we all work to be able to eat, and our food is what allows us to lead our daily existence, to immerse ourselves in important relationships, to fight for the things that matter, to give our little or big contribution to the life of the world. Bread and wine are two symbols par excellence, because they show the unity between God's gift and our own efforts, between our work and that of others, between daily toil and the joy of relationships and celebration. Now in the Mass we offer to the Father all our work and toil and all our hope and joy. We offer them to him not because he needs them or demands them from us, but because the one who loves gives, indeed gives himself. By making this offering, we admit that things, treated simply as such, are a dying world and that communion with this world does not save us. Only by connecting them to God do we receive the gift of life from him.

The Eucharist teaches us to touch the world with love

And indeed, what happens at Mass? We offer everything, and while we offer we implore the Father to send the Holy Spirit to unite our poverty to the offering of Christ, his Son, who came so that each one of us, in him, may become a child of the Father. In this way our bread and wine become Christ, the gift par excellence of the Father, our true brother, in whom we are all brothers and sisters at last and discover ourselves as such.

We believe that the world is for the human person, because it is a gift from the one who loves us and is at the service of the life of God's children, just as each one of us is at the service of others. And just as in the Eucharist bread and wine become Christ because they are bathed by the Spirit, so the whole of creation (people, things, animals, plants, time, and space) becomes a personal word of God when it is used for love, for the good of others, especially those who have need of it.

A great hope

Gift, repentance, offering, fraternity: here are four words that declare a vision of reality and of creation, but that also indicate a path of healing from the need of possession, of power, of abuse toward sharing, collaboration, and respect. In short, toward a universal brotherhood — like the one shown to us by Saint Francis of Assisi — the patron saint of those who work for ecology, true human ecology, because it has the taste of the way God saves the world. This is my great hope for our time.

Francis

NOTES

Preface

[1]Common Declaration of Pope Francis and the Ecumenical Patriarch Bartholomew I, Jerusalem, May 25, 2014, 5–8.

[2]Joint Declaration of His Holiness Bartholomew, Ecumenical Patriarch of Constantinople, of His Beatitude Ieronymos, Archbishop of Athens and All Greece, and of His Holiness Pope Francis, April 16, 2016.

[3]Joint Message of Pope Francis and Ecumenical Patriarch Bartholomew on the World Day of Prayer for Creation, September 1, 2017.

An Integral Vision

[1]Francis, encyclical letter *Laudato Si'*, May 24, 2015, 13.

[2]Ibid., 124.

[3]Video Message of His Holiness Pope Francis on the Occasion of the Meeting of National and International Representatives: "Expo of Ideas 2015 — Toward the Milan Charter," February 7, 2015.

From Momentous Challenge to Global Opportunity

[1]Laudato Si', 23–26.

[2]Ibid., 32–42.

[3]Fifth General Conference of Latin American Bishops, Aparecida document, June 29, 2007, 86.

[4]Conference of the Catholic Bishops of the Philippines, pastoral letter "What is Happening to our Beautiful Land?," January 29, 1988.

[5]Laudato Si', 209–215.

[6]John Paul II, encyclical letter Centesimus Annus, May 1, 1991, 39.

[7]Message for the World Day of Peace, January 1, 1990, 14.

Speeches, Audiences, and Homilies

[1]Homily for the beginning of the Petrine ministry, March 19, 2013.

[2]General Audience, May 21, 2014.

[3]Plenary speech on the occasion of the Second International Conference on Nutrition, November 20, 2014.

[4]Letter of Pope Francis for the establishment of the World Day of Prayer for the Care of Creation, August 6, 2015.

[5]Message for the celebration of the World Day of Prayer for the Care of Creation, September 1, 2016.

[6]Letter of Pope Francis for the establishment of the World Day of Prayer for the Care of Creation.

[7]Address in Santa Barbara, California, November 8, 1997.

[8]Bartholomew I, Message for the Day of Prayer for the Protection of Creation, September 1, 2012.

[9]Address to the Second World Meeting of Popular Movement, Santa Cruz de la Sierra, Bolivia, July 9, 2015.

[10]Third Meditation, Retreat during the Jubilee for Priests, Basilica of Saint Paul Outside the Walls, Rome, June 2, 2016.

[11]General Audience, March 20, 2016.

[12]Bartholomew I, Message for the Day of Prayer for the Protection of Creation, January 1, 1997.

[13]First Meditation, Retreat during the Jubilee for Priests, Basilica of Saint John Lateran, Rome, June 2, 2016.

[14]General Audience, June 30, 2016.

[15]The corporal works of mercy are feeding the hungry, giving drink to the thirsty, clothing the naked, welcoming the stranger, visiting the sick, visiting the imprisoned, burying the dead. The spiritual works of mercy are counseling the doubtful, instructing the ignorant, admonishing sinners, consoling the afflicted, forgiving offenses, bearing patiently those who do us ill, praying for the living and the dead.

[16]Third Meditation, Retreat for the Jubilee for Priests, Basilica of Saint Paul Outside the Walls, Rome, June 2, 2016.

[17]Message of Pope Francis for the 2017 Fraternity Campaign of the Church in Brazil.

[18]Speech at the seminar "The Human Right to Water," February 24, 2017.

[19]Joint Message of Pope Francis and Ecumenical Patriarch Bartholomew on the World Day of Prayer for Creation, September 1, 2017.

[20]Message of Pope Francis for the World Day of Prayer for Care of Creation, September 1, 2018.

[21]Cf. Saint John Paul II, Catechesis of May 7, 1986.

[22]Message of Pope Francis to Participants at Study Day on Water Promoted by the FAO in Madrid, December 13, 2018.

[23]Audience to Participants in the International Conference "Religions and the Sustainable Development Goals (SDGs): Listening to the cry of the earth and of the poor."

[24]When, for example, due to inequalities in the distribution of power, the burden of immense debt is placed on the shoulders of the poor and poor countries, when unemployment is widespread despite the ex-

pansion of trade or when people are simply treated as a means for the growth of others, we need to question fully our key development model. In the same way, when in the name of progress we destroy the source of development — our common home — then the dominant model must be called into question. By questioning this model and reexamining the world economy, participants in the dialogue on development will be able to find an alternative global economic and political system. However, in order for this to happen, we must address the causes of the distortion of development, which is what in recent Catholic social teaching goes by the name of "structural sins." Denouncing such sins is already a good contribution that religions make to the discussion on the world's development. Nonetheless, alongside this denunciation, we must also put forward feasible ways of conversion to people and communities.

[25]Cf. United Nations, Transforming Our World: The 2030 Agenda for Sustainable Development, 2015.

[26]UNESCO, Message from Irina Bokova, Director General of UNESCO, on the occasion of the International Day of the World's Indigenous Peoples, August 9, 2017.

[27]Speech to participants in the meeting promoted by the Department for Integral Human Development Service on the Mining Industry, May 3, 2019.

[28]CELAM, *Missionary Disciples: Custodians of Our Common Home*, 11.

[29]Ibid., 12.

A Great Hope
[1]Cf. John Paul II, encyclical letter *Sollicitudo rei socialis*, 36–40.